BITTERNE & WEST END
THROUGH TIME

HQH

The Hampshire Collection

Hampshire
County Council

CL82 7/02 10k

Bitterne, West End & District Rifle Club

Winners of the Seely Cup and Astor Tankard, 1906. The Astor Tankard is a County Trophy: each English County Association has one, competed for by rifle clubs in that County. The winning team then represents their County in the National Astor Trophy (The Astor County Championships) at Bisley and in the 1906 final the team shown here were placed sixteenth. The team captain was Mr J Bailey, who lived in Chapel Street, Bitterne, and was also the Club Secretary. The club was affiliated to the National Rifle Association with the number 419 and had a declared membership of 42 civilians and two HM Forces. It is suspected that the Seely Cup was won in a local county competition.

BITTERNE &
WEST END
THROUGH TIME

Bitterne and West End
Local History Societies

AMBERLEY PUBLISHING

Acknowledgements

The editorial team of Ian Abrahams, Pauline Berry, Joy Bowyer, Keith Marsh, Nigel Wood and Peter Wallace would like to thank members and friends of our two societies who have generously donated photographs to us, a selection of which we have been able to use in this book. In addition we would like to thank the Southern Daily Echo, Roverang, the Southampton & District Transport Heritage Trust and Southampton City Archives for the use of photographs, and Jim Brown for proof reading the manuscript.

First published 2009

Amberley Publishing Plc
Cirencester Road, Chalford,
Stroud, Gloucestershire, GL6 8PE

www.amberley-books.com

© Bitterne and West End Local History Societies, 2009

The right of Bitterne and West End Local History Societies to be identified as the Authors of this work has been asserted in accordance with the Copyrights, Designs and Patents Act 1988.

British Library Cataloguing in Publication Data.
A catalogue record for this book is available from the British Library.

ISBN 978 1 84868 258 0

Typesetting and Origination by Amberley Publishing.
Printed in Great Britain.

Foreword

When the Bitterne Local History Society was first approached by Amberley Publishing about compiling this book we had concerns about taking on the project. Although our society has a library of over a thousand photographs, we have allowed many of the best to be used in *Then & Now*-type books about Southampton, and we wanted to avoid duplicating the contents of these books. In addition it is only a year since our last book, *The Book of Bitterne*, was published and, although that book was more textual, it also precluded the use of several hundred pictures. However the chance of producing a book showing the changing face of the area over time was exciting, and Amberley's proposals of using sepia for the older images and colour for the more recent, of abandoning the constraints of chapters and of including subjects other than just town scenes, convinced us to proceed.

To widen both the appeal of the book and the selection of pictures available, we decided to invite our friends at the West End Local History Society to join us in the venture to produce *Bitterne & West End Through Time*. We have striven to ensure a balance of pictures across the area with a variety of subjects, including a human element. A few of the pictures have been published before, but not in the context of comparison with more recent times, so we hope these will meet the readers' approval.

Both Bitterne and West End developed as villages during the nineteenth century, prior to which the area was predominantly heath land, interspersed with isolated farms and hamlets. The construction of turnpike roads, the recognition of the fine views afforded from the higher ground and the enclosure of common land led to an influx of gentry, and the tradesmen and labourers to support them. Both villages were originally part of the Parish of South Stoneham, but as their population expanded they were given autonomy as parishes in their own right. Gradually Southampton expanded - with Bitterne Park being absorbed into the County Borough in 1896, Bitterne in 1920, and Harefield and Thornhill in 1954. These are now indistinct districts within the City of Southampton, whilst West End retains its own identity as a Civil Parish within Eastleigh District, although its rural character of 30 years ago is disappearing fast.

With this book we seek to illustrate a few of the many changes that have taken place over the last century. Some of these, such as the construction of housing estates on the former gentries' estates and the division of Bitterne by the bypass, have irreversibly altered the townscape. But a study of the following pictures will reveal more subtle differences as well, changes that have been gradual and have gone previously unnoticed. Enjoy our book!

Bitterne Local History Society

The imminent construction of the Bitterne bypass was the catalyst for the formation of the BLHS in 1981. Local people, keen to ensure that the area's heritage was not lost under the bulldozers, began salvaging items of interest. Letters appeared in the local paper recounting memories of the past, and an exhibition and meeting were arranged: the BLHS was formed.

The society's objective is to promote an interest in local history and to preserve and protect features and items of historic interest. We successfully campaigned to save 602 Bitterne Road (the last cob & thatched cottage in Bitterne) and the statue of the Lion (now in the precinct). We rescue artefacts, collect photographs and documents, organise trips, give talks and guided walks, loan items to schools, and publish books, a series of local papers and a quarterly magazine.

In 1993 we opened our Heritage & Research Centre at 225 Peartree Avenue. The displays are constantly changing, but you are sure to see some amusing and amazing items from days long ago, or perhaps more recent, that might include an early typewriter or teasmade, a church organ, Victorian toys, shop tills in £sd, a gas lamp or a telephone exchange. Wartime memories can be invoked by helmets, gas masks or posters. The recently refurbished research facilities include many local books, street directories, hundreds of maps, thousands of photographs, church magazines and computer databases. These, together with our members' expertise, can assist you with family or local history research related to the area around Bitterne.

The BLHS now have over 250 members worldwide and meet at the United Reformed Church (in Bitterne precinct) at 7.00pm on the second Saturday of each month (excluding August), usually with a guest speaker. For further details of our society please visit our website at www.bitterne.net.

West End Local History Society

The West End Local History Society was established in 1996, yet its main stimulus came with the closure of the fire station in West End when the cover it provided was transferred to a new fire station at Hightown. The Old Fire Station, on the corner of Orchards Way and High Street, became a community building and the property of West End Parish Council, and the fledgling society set up a museum there in 1997.

The Museum & Heritage Centre is now open on Saturdays between 10am and 4pm, staffed by volunteers and has excellent research facilities covering the West End and Moorgreen area.

Monthly meetings of the society are held on the first Wednesday evening of each month at 7.30pm (except August) in the nearby Parish Centre in Chapel Road, with guest speakers covering such diverse topics as 'Moorgreen Workhouse', 'The Buildings of Hampshire'. 'The Liners of Southampton', 'The Itchen Navigation' and 'The Flying Boats of Southampton'.

Our free newsletter *Westender* is issued bi-monthly at these meetings and is also available on our web site at www.westendlhs.hampshire.org.uk. You can also contact us by email at westendlhs@aol.com.

The Red Lion Public House and Bursledon Road, Bitterne

The wedding cortège of Miss Amy Macnaghten of Bitterne Manor and Lieutenant Evelyn Culme-Seymour of Glenville leaving the parish church on 29 May 1908 amid throngs of local children. In November 2008 the road is quiet again, road traffic having been re-routed along the bypass in 1984.

West End Fire Station

Auxiliary and National Fire Service crews with the Dennis New World fire appliance at the opening of the fire station in May 1939 by Mrs Pearson of Oaklands, Allington Lane. A young Rodney Whale, standing with the crew, presented her with a bouquet. Today the building is the West End Local History Museum and Heritage Centre.

The junction of Somerset Avenue and Bitterne Road East, Bitterne

Harefield was a country estate from the building of Harefield House in 1846 until its destruction by fire in May 1917, following which it was purchased by Edwin Jones & Co Ltd. A few areas of the estate were sold off for housing in the 1920s, with development of the remainder starting in the late 1930s by private builders, and being continued after the Second World War by Southampton Council. The views shown here illustrate how little this junction has changed since August 1950.

The parade of shops in West End High Street

A pre-war view of a section of the High Street with W G Wiltshire's newsagents, built for him by Haines Bros in 1927. Note the thatch-roofed cottage on the left, one of several remaining in the village at that time. Today the shops remain but with different occupants.

A classroom at Harefield Primary School, Yeovil Chase

The picture taken soon after the school opened in 1957 shows a typical classroom of the era: wooden chairs, straight rows of desks with lift-up lids and ink-wells, regimented notice boards and the usual lighting and flooring of the period. Today these have been replaced by a much more welcoming and stimulating environment, whilst the houses opposite are now obscured by the trees of the sensory play trail.

West End High Street and New Road crossroads

A group of Sunday School children, *The Young Hopefuls* outside Langford's Provision Stores which served as a Post and Telegraph Office about 1905. It was replaced by a new building, initially a bank and now a toy shop.

The Bitterne fork, where Bursledon Road joins Bitterne Road

This busy junction was often grid-locked, as in the picture of the mid-1970s, which also shows the old school, Harry Guster's hardware shop (which closed in March 1976) and a branch of local entrepreneur Bob Sperring's newsagency empire. The same view in November 2008 shows the new weekly market that takes place in the precinct each Wednesday. The shop on the left is still a newsagents, whilst the school and Guster's have been replaced by the United Reformed Church with shops underneath.

Quob Farm House, West End

Rebuilt early in the twentieth century, this farmhouse in Quob Lane once belonged to Fred Woolley JP, twice Mayor of Southampton, who renamed it Burnmoor Farm. During the Second World War the steel cable of a runaway barrage balloon demolished the ornate conservatory. Renamed Quob Farm and converted into flats, it is now surrounded by a housing estate.

Thornhill Park estate, now known as 'bungalow town'

Like Harefield, Thornhill Park was a large country estate on which the building of houses and bungalows began before the Second World War. The first area to be developed was to the north and the abundance of bungalows resulted in its local nickname. After the war council housing was built on the remainder of the estate, including three 14-storey blocks of flats built in 1964, two of which can be seen on the skyline of the modern view, taken in the vicinity of the earlier picture.

Hatch Farm, West End

The farmhouse pictured with members of the Fray family at the turn of the twentieth century, when it was surrounded by over 200 acres of arable and pastureland. Albert Fray, the tenant farmer looking over the hedge, died in 1905 whilst working on the farm. The colour photograph, taken in the 1980's, shows the farmhouse prior to its demolition around 1990. Larch Close now occupies its site.

The Target Public House and footbridge, Bursledon Road, Sholing

Built by Brickwoods in 1939 as a 'family pub' on the corner of Butts Road, with landlord Edward McLachlan in charge, it became a Whitbread house in 1971. The footbridge across the busy Bursledon Road which can also be seen in the picture taken around 2000 *(Mark Lawrence)* had already gone by the time The Target was demolished in 2007, to be replaced by a block of flats which the architect based on the pub's style and footprint.

Midlands Corner, West End

A view of the bottom of Church Hill and Chalk Hill (formerly known as South Road) around 1905, showing Woodleigh (later SGB House) with its verandah. The house has since been demolished for redevelopment, whilst after extensive widening and road re-alignment, traffic has now taken over the A27.

2nd Southampton (Bitterne) Company Boys Brigade

The Company form up in Pound Street before marching to the Congregational Church, around 1961. The lads at the front are Derek Saunders (left), standard bearer David Trussler, and Jim Ramshaw (who is still in the brigade after 55 years service). Alongside them is the children's playground, traces of which can still be seen. On 2 June 2007 the band played on the roof of the United Reformed Church for the wedding of Anthea Moyle and Jonathan Wedge.

Swaythling Road, West End

A tranquil pre-First World War scene showing the old forge and cottage on the corner of Allington Lane, now Romill Close. The reputed 'Thousand Year Old Oak' can be seen opposite but alas it has long since gone. Now no longer a forge, the building is now used as the workshops for a car sales business.

West End Road, Bitterne

In 1906 West End Road was little more than a leafy country lane. The horse trough, now relocated, was paid for by public subscription and erected in 1905 to refresh horses after the climb up Lances Hill. The horse and cart are delivering bread from the Alexandra Bakery, Sholing, for Lankester & Crook. In the distance the road can just be seen passing the recreation ground, whilst in the 2008 view it has become the bridge over the bypass. The shop on the right was Sports Cycle Shop for many years, then more recently Pam's Greengrocers.

Gater's Mill, West End

A riverside scene showing Gater's Mill on the River Itchen, taken prior to the big fire of October 1917, when the mill was totally gutted. Today the tall trees hide the rebuilt mill now used for business premises. There have been mills on this site since the thirteenth and fourteenth century, comprising cloth, paper and corn production at various times.

Bitterne Carnival

Until recent times carnivals have been a popular form of entertainment and helped foster real community spirit. The older picture shows the float of the Court Rose of Bitterne outside the Red Lion's stables in Church Road, now Bursledon Road, around 1910. The carnival was revived as a 'walking carnival' for a few years in the 1980 and 1990s, and the colour photograph shows the Carnival Princess being paraded through the precinct about 1992.

Amateur dramatics in West End

Taken about 1916 on Hatch Grange, the earlier photograph shows the cast of 'Zuleika', including local schoolmaster George Elliott, holding a book. The colour picture shows the cast of 'No Time for Fig Leaves', a 1991 production by West End Little Theatre Club.

SOUTHAMPTON GARDEN SUBURB.

The River Itchen from the Chessel Estate, Bitterne

A prime reason for the establishment of so many gentry's houses in Bitterne was the fine views given from the high ground, across Southampton and the New Forest to the Isle of Wight. One of these was Chessel House, once home to David Lance and visited by Jane Austen. The extensive grounds of this house were built on in the 1920s and 1930s, the estate being marketed as the Southampton Garden Suburb and resulting in many more people enjoying the splendid views.

South Stoneham Union Workhouse, West End

Little has changed outwardly in the appearance of the South Stoneham Union Workhouse in Botley Road from the early 20th century to present, except for the name and purpose of the buildings. Built around 1848-50, it is now known as Moorgreen Hospital (NHS) and the future of its Victorian buildings is uncertain.

The Bitterne Brewery, West End Road, Bitterne

Two Royal Blue charabancs ready to depart from the Bitterne Brewery on a men's day trip; note the ladders for embarkation along their side! The building on the left was the brewery, which ceased brewing before the First World War, and became a charabanc garage until demolished in 1926. The pub was badly damaged, and landlord William Sly fatally wounded in the blitz, but it continued to trade and was rebuilt in 1952, since when it has been refurbished and renamed several times.

West End football teams

Our picture shows West End Rovers taken in 1910 with Edwin Stephens, far right in the front row. As a comparison, there is one taken of the local team during the 1953-54 season.

Misselbrook's Car Sales, Bitterne

Many Bitterne people will remember Tom Misselbrook's car sales in Bitterne Road, adjacent to Lion Place, which he started as a spin-off from his Bitterne Cab Company in 1945. The mid-1950s picture shows Tom (second from right) with a selection of cars of the time, including Ford Populars, a Morris Minor, Austin A30 and A40s, and a Standard Flying 12. When the bypass was built the business was relocated to the corner of Maybray King Way and Bursledon Road. Tom, who was president of the BLHS, passed away in June 2008.

Hickley Farm, West End

The picture taken in 1915 shows the tenant farmer Mr Charles Reeves standing in the doorway of Hickley Farmhouse. Today's picture shows the location but the farmhouse has long gone and the farm is now the site of The Rose Bowl, home of Hampshire County Cricket.

Bitterne Scouts at camp

The aim of the Scout movement is the same today as it was when Baden-Powell first took lads to camp on Brownsea Island in 1907, although methods have had to adapt to a changing world. The khaki uniforms and bell tents of the camp at Warsash in about 1932, are now consigned to history, it being necessary to modernise equipment and provide more adventurous activities. Canoeing formed a major part of the programme of the Troop's summer camp at Marlow, August 2008.

The Choir of St James' Church, West End

The Choir of St James' Church with the Revd Dr Ivor Jeffery-Machin (who was Vicar between 1943-53) and several well-known local residents including members of the Fray family. The colour picture shows the choir in 2006 with the present Vicar, Revd Brian Pickett, standing at the back on the right.

Shales, West End Road, Bitterne

One of many large houses built in the area about 1840, Shales was owned by an admiral, a bishop, two colonels, an MP and a JP. The house was renamed Langstaff House in 1910, then St Theresa's in 1946. A large extension, built in the 1960s, still exists in Edelvale Road and is now called St Theresa's, whilst the original Shales was demolished in 1984 and replaced by St Francis House, with St Francis Avenue built on part of the grounds.

Parish Church of St James, West End

The original church was built between 1836-38, but unfortunately the spire was struck by lightning in 1875 and subsequently demolished, while the tower was made waterproof with a small hipped roof as seen in this photograph of 1880. In 1890 the church was totally rebuilt without a tower, as seen in the 2008 picture.

Shales Road, Bitterne

Charles Dewey's Standard car in Shales Road, known locally as Back Lane because it led to the tradesmen's entrance to the Harefield estate. The building in the background is Shalom, part of Redcote Convent. Since the 1970s houses have been built on much of the convent's grounds, including here in Shales Road, yet Shalom remains. The bus is a Dennis Dart of First Bus, operating the popular 'Bitterne Hoppa' service of three looped routes around Bitterne, providing a lifeline to the less mobile people of the area, and often picking them up at their gate.

The Sportsman's Arms, West End

The picture dating from the 1930's shows the Sportsman's Arms, demolished and rebuilt as The Sportsman just before the Second World War. This building was demolished in 2003 to make way for Fielders Court, the retirement homes shown in the colour picture.

The Elephant & Castle, Bursledon Road, Sholing

The Elephant & Castle was built in the 1930s on the site of an earlier pub dating from the 1860s, and nicknamed The Old Black House because of its corrugated iron walls and black tarpaulin roof. Once it was a Mew Langton's pub (the adjacent land was the Mew Langton's sports ground) but by the 1980s when it was refurbished as a Roast Inn, it had become part of the Whitbread Group. The earlier picture *(Mark Lawrence)* was taken before the protracted campaign to keep the pub open failed with its closure in 2005.

High Street, West End looking east

This view looking up the High Street to Shotters Hill was taken in the early 1900's before the roads were surfaced. The Old National School building is on the left, serving as the Parish Hall. Note the lack of traffic, unlike today's view of this busy village centre.

The junction of Bitterne Road and Athelstan Road, Bitterne Manor

Along with many of the houses on the Chessel Estate, the shops on the corner of Athelstan Road and Bitterne Road were built about 1934 by local builders Armstead & Co, whose offices were in the single-storey unit on the right; the other shops were Roland Minns butchers, Stella (D & R Davis) gowns, Stella (D & R Davis) confectioners, and Herbert Maltby hardware. Only one shop now remains, a pizza take-away.

West End Parish Councillors

Our earlier 1930's picture shows the West End Parish Council under the chairmanship of Cllr Harry Haines seated centre front (who served the community for over 40 years). The recent picture taken in 2006 shows the councillors with the present chairman, Cllr Neville Dickinson, wearing his chain of office.

The junction of Beauworth Avenue and West End Road, Harefield

The view of October 1950 shows the beginning of the council development of Harefield Estate. West End Road crosses the foreground whilst Beauworth Avenue drops into the valley, following the route of the track to Harefield Farm, which stood where the shops in Melchet Road are now.

The Blacksmiths Arms, High Street, West End

An idyllic view of one of the village's public houses, aptly named after its close proximity to the village forge, situated opposite Hatch Grange. The photograph taken about 1900 shows the chequerboard brickwork, later rebuilt after a road traffic accident partially demolished the frontage. Now the building is a private residence which faces an improved road surface that has been much altered and built up over the years.

Looking west along Thornhill Park Road, Thornhill

Thornhill Park Stores is now just another house, but in the 1930s it was a grocery store and tea garden. An enamel sign proudly announces 'You may telephone from here', whilst boards at the roadside advertise Wills' Star and Players' Weights cigarettes.

Shotters Hill, West End

A view of Shotters Hill taken around 1910 shows two of the well-built houses which Haines Bros constructed all over West End. The house on the left, called Homeleigh, was the home of Harry Haines, a well-known member of the community. Today only one of these buildings survives as Pearson's Estate Agents' office.

The junction of Mousehole Lane and Glenfield Avenue, Bitterne

Glenfield Farm stood at the junction of Mousehole Lane and Glenfield Avenue in an area that was inhabited before Bitterne was classed as a village. The earlier picture dates from the 1930s when development of the Glen Valley began.

The White Swan Public House, Mansbridge

A tranquil 1911 Edwardian scene on the River Itchen depicting the pleasure gardens of The White Swan at Mansbridge. Today's view shows a much changed and enlarged building with the riverbank now somewhat overgrown and no sign of rowing boats for hire.

Bitterne Railway Station, Bitterne Manor

The station opened in March 1866 as Bitterne Road Station, so called in typical LSWR fashion, due to its distance from the village. The engine shown in the early 1960s picture is a British Railways standard class 4, but steam trains were soon to be replaced by diesel-electric multiple units, in turn replaced when the line was electrified in 1990.

St James' School, West End

A view of St James' School taken about 1910. Built by Haines Bros builders of West End, it remains little changed today except for the extension added to the far end of the building in 1914 (note the extra gable ends in the colour photograph). Today it still serves the village as the Hilldene Community Centre.

Lances Hill Toll House, Bitterne Road West

Bitterne Road was opened as a turnpike road by the Northam Bridge Company in 1799, with toll gates at Northam Bridge, Hedge End and Lances Hill. The toll gate on the hill was moved three times as housing development enabled it to be avoided and 253 Bitterne Road was the final position, the toll being freed in 1929. The large window on the corner gave sight of traffic approaching the gate, whilst the long porch protected the toll collector during bad weather. The earlier picture is from the 1920s (*Jeff Pain*).

The Methodist Chapel, West End

Members of the congregation outside the Methodist Chapel, built in 1846, at the junction of Chapel Road and Lower New Road photographed about 1960. Bert Haines, in the centre of the group holding his hat, is a member of the local building family. The Chapel was demolished soon after being sold in 1964 and the site is now occupied by modern housing.

Buses in Peartree Avenue, Bitterne

A Leyland Cub KPO/3 bus, built in 1935 and operated by Southampton Corporation in their familiar red and cream livery until 1955, is seen here at the bus stop near Gainsford Road. The scene is repeated in 2008 with Volvo B7TL operated by First Bus who bought out CityBus, the company formed when the Southampton City Transport department was deregulated.

Fray's Stores, West End

The picture of the R F Fray & Co store comes from a postcard dated 1930. Previously the store and bakery were run by G E May. Today the original premises, built by Haines Bros in 1886-87, have been replaced by a new building occupied by Sizzlers and a Tesco Express.

Chapel Street, Bitterne Village

A view looking north along Chapel Street, one of the oldest roads in the village, so named because it once held three chapels: Congregational, Wesleyan Methodist and Baptist. In 1924 the street was renamed Dean Road to avoid confusion with Chapel Road in Southampton, into which Bitterne had been incorporated in 1920; obviously the person who titled the early 1900s postcard was confused!

West End's War Memorial

The early picture shows the unveiling of the memorial on Saturday 5 June 1920 at the corner of High Street and Cemetery Road (now part of West End Road). Brigadier General Harrison and Colonel E K Perkins presided and the Revd F R Dawson led the service. Today the memorial has two name tablets to cover both the First and Second World Wars.

Bitterne Sports Ground, Wynter Road, Harefield

Bitterne Sports Ground was established in the 1920s on part of Shales Flats, parkland to the southwest of Harefield House, and the first part of the estate to be sold for redevelopment. It has hosted many events since, including the Girl Guides rally pictured in the 1950s, various athletics events, local football league matches and the 1991 Bitterne Carnival fête, also seen here.

The Old National School, West End

The original National School building, built in 1838, was serving as the Parish Hall for West End in 1915 when this picture was taken, the school having moved to larger premises, next to the Old Burial Ground beyond Shotters Hill, in 1904. Today the building has long gone and modern stores occupy the site on the corner of Chapel Road and High Street.

Delivering Bitterne's milk

One of the few delivery services that has not completely vanished is the milkman, though it has changed dramatically since these lads delivered milk for James Bailey around 1905. They are pictured in Chapel Street (now Dean Road) outside Bailey's Dairy and Eastman's Butchers; the shops are now gone but the tree to the left is still there! Horse-drawn carts were replaced by pedestrian-controlled handcarts then by electric milk floats, as used by the ever-cheerful Keith Bull, a popular milkman in the district in the 1990s.

The Tennis Club, West End

A 1930's view of the West End Lawn Tennis Club, which stood next to the Parish Church of St James, and is now the site of a small modern housing development, Hatherell Close, named after the first Vicar of West End.

TRAM TERMINUS, COBDEN BRIDGE, BITTERNE PK.

Bitterne Park Triangle and Cobden Bridge

The first Cobden Bridge was built in 1883 by the National Liberal Land Company, owners of much of the land at Bitterne Park. Many of the nearby roads are named after prominent Liberals of the time, including Richard Cobden. The tram from Southampton terminated here until 1923 when the line was extended down Bullar Road. The shops were built about 1911 whilst the clock tower was moved here from Above Bar Street during 1934/35.

West End Village Shop

This photograph of around 1910 is of a village general store in Chapel Road run by Miss Jane May, then later by Cyril Hassell. The freehold was owned by Daniel Haines and was sold in 1919 after his death. Today the location is the site of Chapel Close and a bungalow is situated on the corner of the road.

Lion Place, Bitterne

Lion Place was built in the 1840s and was Bitterne's first shopping centre in what was then the High Street. Originally consisting of four shops, Lankester & Crook extended their shop, which explains why the stone lion adorning the roof is off-centre, as seen in the picture of about 1978. It is not known if the lion was new when the shops were built, but its antiquity led to the BLHS campaigning for its preservation and re-erection in the precinct. The site is now under the road, but is recalled in the tile mosaics in the subways.

The West End Brewery, High Street, West End

An interesting 1920's view of charabancs parked outside The West End Brewery, run by The Winchester Brewery company in the High Street. The view today is somewhat different!

Lances Hill Garage, Bitterne Village

It is hard to believe that it was permissible to dispense petrol through hoses across the pavement and this in the centre of Bitterne! The photograph, dating from the early 1930s, shows the Lances Hill Garage selling Regent petrol at 1s 4d (1/4 that is 7p!) a gallon. W R Holden took over the garage in 1948 and became a seed merchant when a tightening of Health & Safety rules curtailed petrol sales around 1960. The three-storey parade of shops to the right was built in the 1950s and originally included Bitterne's first self-service supermarket, Fine Fare.

Homeleigh, High Street, West End

Here a 1910 photograph shows Homeleigh in the High Street, once home of Harry Haines of the building firm and a parish councillor for many years. It is still recognisable today but now serves as offices of Pearsons' Estate Agents.

Cross Road, Chessel, Bitterne

A Guy Arab III bus of Southampton Corporation Transport slides on the ice in Cross Road and knocks the top off a lamp post, 26 January 1954. In the background is the heavy breakdown crane bought by SCT from the War Dept in 1946. Bus routes through Chessel were always operated by single-deckers because of the gradients, but occasionally double-deckers were diverted if Lances Hill was impassable.

The Corner Shop, Chapel Road, West End

This early twentieth century photograph of the general store on the corner of Chapel Road and High Street has had a series of owners over the years but is still recognisable today, now run by the well-known charity Vitalise. Some windows and a doorway have been bricked up as shown in the current picture.

Merry Oak School, Merry Oak

Opened in 1935 as a co-educational secondary school serving the Bitterne and Sholing communities, it became a boys' school in 1945 when Sholing Girls' School opened. Here the lads of Form IB are doing physical training on the playground between the technical block (pictured) and the school hall. The latter was retained when the school was closed and demolished, and now serves as the community centre, whilst housing occupies the rest of the site.

The Moorgreen Inn, Moorgreen

Latterly run by Mr & Mrs Goodeve, The Moorgreen Inn, seen here in the 1930's with Mr Topp's cottage in the background, dated back to the nineteenth century and was in Moorgreen Road opposite today's Monarch Way. One of several public houses to have disappeared, both The Moorgreen Inn and the cottage have since been replaced by housing.

Pound Street, Bitterne Village

Another of Bitterne's oldest roads, being laid out following the local Act of Enclosure in 1812 and originally called Pound Lane; the pound was situated at the road's junction with the High Street (now Bitterne Road). The views are looking south, with the spire of the parish church just visible over the roofs of the cottages, many of which are still there in 2008, 100 years after the earlier view. Photographers no longer attract an audience!

Youth activities in West End

A group photograph of the West End Company of the Boys Brigade outside the old Parish Hall in 1935. Today's facilities for young people are provided by the Parish Council at the Youth House Young People's Centre in Moorgreen Road.

Looking south along Dean Road, Bitterne Village

A cycling group pictured in Dean Road about 1928. All but one of the row of houses, as well as the Drill Hall at the end, were demolished when the bypass was built, most being replaced by the leisure centre car park. The one house that escaped demolition then was 11 Dean Road which the owners, Claude and Marie Diaper, argued was not required. It was demolished in 2002 following Marie's death, and Cairn Court built on the site.

Moorgreen Road, West End

A 1930's view looking along a very rural Moorgreen Road, with The Moorgreen Inn public house in the middle of the picture. Today the road has changed considerably, by housing development and being crossed by the M27 motorway, built in the 1980s.

The Drill Hall, Bitterne Village

The Drill Hall was behind The Red Lion, alongside Red Lion Cut, and was built around 1910 to replace an earlier wooden building as the headquarters of No 6 Company, Hants 1st Volunteers, Royal Artillery. It was also used for local events: here the Bitterne trades-people aim to raise £150 for the Royal South Hants and Borough Hospitals. When the Margam Hall opened in Merry Oak in 1939 the Drill Hall's military purpose ended, and it then had various occupiers before being demolished in 1982.

The New Inn, West End

The photograph taken around 1905 on the village green outside The New Inn, shows the Bitterne & West End Brass Band, the Independent Order of Oddfellows members wearing their regalia and local people celebrating. A block of apartments known as Rosemount Court, named after the house originally next door, today occupies the site of the inn whilst the village green has disappeared with road changes and widening.

Bitterne Cubs at the Gordon Hall, Brook Road

The 3rd Itchen (Bitterne) Wolf Cubs, pictured at the back of the Martin Hall in 1932, with Cub Mistress Ethel (Kim) Gordon on the left. Previously called the Martin Hall, it was built by the Martin family as a 'workmen's hall' in 1881, and was renamed to honour the Gordon family in 1969. As can be seen in the colour picture taken in the upstairs hall, the Cubs uniform and badges have changed since 1932, but the neckerchiefs and broad smiles are the same!

Hatch Farm Cottages in Chapel Road, West End

An early twentieth century photograph of Hatch Farm cottages in Chapel Road, the middle terrace houses the small village shop run by Miss Jane May. Today a mixture of houses and bungalows occupy the site.

The Castle, Witts Hill, Midanbury

The gothic 'castle' was actually the gateway and lodge to the large country mansion, Midanbury House, and was a copy of that to the Blaise Castle estate in Bristol. It fell into disuse from 1913, and the pub was built on the site in 1935 by Coopers Brewery, to serve the inhabitants of the then developing Midanbury area.

Merry Gardens, Chapel Road, West End

Originally owned by the Fray family and built around 1907, Merry Gardens, which was named after a cherry orchard that once stood on the site, has changed quite dramatically. Today it is called Highview House.

Brewery Road, Bitterne Village

Brewery Road was so named because of its proximity to The Bitterne Brewery, though brewing ceased there before the First World War. In both the 1904 and modern views, Brook Road can be seen going off to the right, whilst the stream that gave it its name is culverted under Brewery Road in the dip. Brewery Road became part of Dean Road in 1924. The numerous hedgerows around the village contribute to its rural character and many are protected by preservation orders.

The Old Burial Ground, West End

An early twentieth century view of the Old Burial Ground at the top of Shotters Hill, showing the ornate railings surrounding the plot of the Fletcher family, who once owned the Hatch Grange estate. Today the railings and stone curb have long gone but the memorials remain.

The Sand Pit, Bitterne Village

The recreation ground between West End Road and Pound Street, February 1979. Under the local Act of Enclosure, this plot of land was allotted to the villagers for the extraction of sand for building purposes, so when the resulting pit was later levelled to form the recreation ground it was still known to locals as The Sand Pit. A distinctive local landmark prominent in the older picture is the Roman Catholic Church's tower which was demolished in 2008.

High Street, WestEnd, Nr. Southampton.

5129

High Street, West End, looking west

A view of the High Street photographed around 1910 looking towards the old Parish Hall on the corner of Chapel Road. The West End Brewery public house was later demolished and a new one constructed at the rear. Today the site is the car park in front of the present West End Brewery, set in a much altered High Street.

The Roverang Show

The senior sections of the Scout and Guide movements in the Itchen Districts performed their first 'gang show' for one night only, in March 1957 at Middle Road Girls' School; the older picture is of the 1960 production, 'Flying High'. During the next few years the show evolved into a week of performances. Costumes, music and choreography became more elaborate, and 'youngsters' were added. For most of the last 40 years the show has been staged at the Nuffield Theatre, and the colour picture shows some of the cast and the orchestra during a Stock, Aitkin & Waterman tribute in the 2008 show.

Langfords Corner, West End

A 1910 photograph of J N Langford's Grocery Store on the corner of Upper New Road and High Street, which also served as the Post, Telegraph and Telephone Office for the village. Today the site is occupied by a different building housing a toy shop.

Yeovil Chase, Harefield

Yeovil Chase follows a former track on the Harefield estate, as seen in the picture of May 1949. The council houses were built in 1950 and the schools on the left, which are on the site of the Queens Athletic Association's playing field, in 1957. After Harefield House, the site of which is further along Yeovil Chase, was destroyed by fire the estate was bought by Edwin Jones & Co Ltd who farmed it and used it for staff recreation.

Civil Defence in West End

The West End Civil Defence volunteers photographed in the late 1940s on the tennis courts which were behind the old wooden church hall on Church Hill next to St James' Church. Both the Civil Defence organisation, church hall and tennis courts have vanished and the site is now occupied by a car park for the church.

Bitterne shopping centre

A snowy day in January 1982, looking east from outside Sainsburys, with F W Woolworth's first shop in Bitterne on the left. The buildings have not changed since, Sainsbury's is the only shop that has remained, though considerably enlarged. The main difference of course is the removal of the traffic on to the bypass in 1984, following which the road through the centre of Bitterne became a pedestrian precinct.

Lower New Road, West End

A view of Lower New Road from around 1906, with a carrier's horse-drawn vehicle making a delivery. The view today is similar except for the motor cars and surfaced road.

Decorating the house

15 and 17 Brook Road, Bitterne, decorated for the coronation of King Edward VII in August 1902. Entertainment then was mainly home-made, people decorating their homes with flags and bunting in order to join in national festivities. After all, they couldn't watch them on television! Nowadays Christmas is about the only time when houses are decorated, relying heavily on coloured lights. For over ten years residents of Broadwater Road, Townhill Park have turned their road into a twinkling wonderland, typified by Dave Sainsbury's house.

The Oddfellows in West End

A group photograph of the West End branch of the Independent Order of Oddfellows wearing full regalia outside The New Inn about 1930. Today the site has been redeveloped and is host to Rosemount Court, an apartment block.

The old Bitterne Schools

After the Second World War, Bitterne School became the first in Southampton to have its own dining hall, shown to the right of this photograph taken about 1950 soon after it opened. The Junior School (built in 1856) is to the left whilst the Queen Victoria Infants School (built in 1897) is in the centre. The flat concrete-roofed extensions are air raid shelters. Following the relocation of the schools in 1978 the area was redeveloped as shops with the United Reformed Church above and service area (seen here) at the rear.

Haines Bros Builders' Yard, West End

The third generation of Haines brothers, Bert on the far left and Roy on the far right, with two of their employees outside their builders' yard and office in the High Street, around 1930. The site is occupied today by the Post Office and adjoining shops.

Maytree Road, Bitterne

Maytree Road was a small cul-de-sac off the High Street with terraced houses on each side. On the corners were the Carpenters Arms (where Sainsburys is now) and The Ritz Cinema (latterly the bowling alley). When Sainsburys first opened in 1965 deliveries were to a loading bay in Maytree Road, but this moved to the rear when the shop expanded in 1972.

The Wheelwright's Cottage, Chalk Hill, West End

An early twentieth century photograph of the wheelwrights thatched cottage in Chalk Hill (previously known as South Road). The cottage dates back to the mid seventeenth century and still exists, although extended both sides and sub-divided into two cottages today.

Mrs Guy's Cottage, Bitterne Village

Standing opposite Bitterne School, Mrs Guy operated a tuck shop from her thatched cottage in Bitterne High Street. Gradually the fields around were built on, so it was inevitable that the cob cottage would be demolished and it was replaced about 1935 by Bitterne Parade. To the right the timbered building was Hornby's Bitterne Dairy for many years (now Haytons florist), whilst Boyes Bakery is advertising Hovis.